The Wonder of Prenatal Education has been a real eye opener for me. I am expecting my second child and I have found the information in this book practical and well explained. It has given me knowledge I didn't have in my previous pregnancy, which is based on scientific fact.

— **Lisa Birch**, *A second time expecting mom*

Believe it or not, everything starts in the womb. A pregnancy's full potential can be reached through a careful analysis and adjustment of the mother's external and mental world... "*Your Baby's Developing Brain*" Series by Dr. Chong Chen is a great resource to add to your knowledge about the way we function as humans and how to assist future tiny humans to reach their best physical and psychological potential.

— **Lucia Grosaru**, *Psychology Corner*

Your Baby's Developing Brain Series III

THE WONDER OF PRENATAL EDUCATION

Why You Should Listen to Mozart and Sing to Your Baby While Pregnant

CHONG CHEN, PH.D.

Brain & Life Publishing

London

ISBN 978-1-9997601-0-6 E-book

ISBN 978-1-9997601-5-1 Paperback

Brain & Life Publishing

27 Old Gloucester Street, London, U.K.

First Printing, 2017

For information about special needs for bulk purchases, sales promotions, and educational needs, please contact orders@brainandlife.net.

ALSO BY CHONG CHEN

Plato's Insight: How Physical Exercise Boosts Mental Excellence

Fitness Powered Brains: Optimize Your Productivity, Leadership and Performance

Psychology for Pregnancy: How Your Mental Health during Pregnancy Programs Your Baby's Developing Brain (Your Baby's Developing Brain Series I)

The Seed of Intelligence: Boost Your Baby's Developing Brain through Optimal Nutrition and Healthy Lifestyle (Your Baby's Developing Brain Series II)

I wish I could take a quiet corner in the heart of my baby's very own world.

I know it has stars that talk to him, and a sky that stoops down to his face to amuse him with its silly clouds and rainbows.

— Rabindranath Tagore, *Baby's World*

To my parents for their love and support

Table of Contents

PREFACE

This series was originally written for my family and friends. Given my training in medicine, psychiatry, and brain science, they had long been asking me what science says about pregnancy and parenting. For instance, how does one boost a baby's brain development? How can one raise a genius? Is there anything parents can do during pregnancy to ensure a healthy, intelligent, and happy child? To answer their questions, I decided to do extensive research myself. After all, I am a scientist. Now, after over six years of research, I have finally completed this comprehensive report.

My primary interest lies in brain development. There are already many popular books on how to promote the physical health of babies but brain development, in contrast, is only a recent scientific topic of discussion. Our brain determines our intellectual, emotional, and social functioning. The latter defines who we are. As Rene Descartes put it, "I think, therefore I am." That's it.

I have gone through all the necessary medical training in gynecology (the medical field dealing with female reproductive systems), obstetrics (pregnancy and childbirth) and pediatrics (the care of infants and children). Yet, I myself was astonished by the results of my research. Parents' health and behaviors, which may seem subtle to themselves, exert a powerful and lost-lasting impact on their infant's developing brain and some of that impact persists well into adulthood. Consequently, I feel that the results of my research should be available to every parent.

Then came this series, "*Your Baby's Developing Brain.*" The first three volumes of this series focus on the period of pregnancy. They are about what parents can do during pregnancy to protect and boost their baby's developing brain. The first volume focuses on the psychological health of the parents during pregnancy, and is titled *Psychology for Pregnancy: How Your Mental Health during Pregnancy Programs Your Baby's Developing Brain*. The second volume introduces a healthy maternal lifestyle, including proper nutrition and sleep, etc., and is titled *The Seed of Intelligence: Boost Your Baby's Developing Brain through Optimal Nutrition and Healthy Lifestyle*. The third volume, namely the present book, focuses on antenatal education or taijiao, i.e., educating babies in the womb. I have planned more volumes on postpartum parenting and if you want to be notified when a new volume is released, please sign up for my newsletter at https://brainandlife.net.

PART 1: THE INTELLIGENT FETUS

1. A newborn's preference

She said, "This time I'm gonna get ya," simultaneously poising her hand over the baby's belly ready to begin a finger-tickle-march up the baby's belly and into the hilarious recesses of his neck and armpits. As she hovered and spoke, he smiled and squirmed but always stayed in eye contact with her.

— Daniel N. Stern, *The First Relationship* (1977)

Even just after birth, an infant shows robust intelligent behavior. They prefer their mother's voice over other female voices. They also prefer their native language over foreign languages.

Psychologist Anthony J. DeCasper and William P. Fifer at the University of North Carolina at Greensboro are two pioneers in the study of newborns' behavior. In the 1980s, they devised a nonnutritive sucking paradigm. In this still widely used paradigm, newborn infants are given a feeding contraption attached to a tape recorder. If the babies suck fast they can hear one set of sounds through headphones. If they suck slow, they can hear a different set of sounds.

With this paradigm, DeCasper and Fifer discovered that within hours of birth, a baby prefers their mother's voice to a stranger's: they tended to suck to hear their own mother. Furthermore, two-day-old infants of monolingual English or Spanish speakers prefer their native language. They sucked in a way to hear audio recordings of female strangers speaking their native language. English infants sucked to hear English while Spanish infants sucked to hear Spanish. Thus, newborns possess the ability to differentiate their mother's voice from other women's voice and their native language from foreign languages.

More recently, in a 2009 study, Kathleen Wermke at the University of Wurzburg, Germany, analyzed the spontaneous crying patterns of German and French newborns during changing diapers and before feeding. Despite being merely 2–5 days old, these infants cried in a melody that was consistent with the intonation of their native language. German infants preferentially cried with a falling melody contour, whereas French infants preferentially cried with a rising contour. The melody of their native language has an imprint in the infants' brain. When crying, the infants are unconsciously affected by this imprint.

The newborn infants have had only minimal exposure to their mother's voice and their native language after birth: they are just several hours to days old. Thus, they may have learned and remembered the voice and language pattern before birth, that is, while still in the womb. In order for this "fetal learning" phenomenon to be possible, three conditions must be met:

- There must be detectable sound in the womb: at least the mother's voice and speech should be readily perceivable.

- The fetus must be able to hear: their ears should be fully functional at some time point during pregnancy.

- The fetus must have the ability to learn and remember, albeit not necessarily consciously: they should be able to store the sound they hear in their memory.

But how are these conditions met? We will examine each condition in turn in the next three chapters.

2. Your baby's auditory world: sounds in the womb

If you put your hand over your mouth and speak, that's very similar to the situation the fetus is in.

— Eino Partanen (2013)

Occasionally, in order to induce or accelerate labor, a midwife or obstetrician will artificially rupture the membrane with a specialized tool. Over three decades ago, using this kind of method, several scientists recorded sounds from within the human uterus after the artificial rupture of membranes. It turns out that the uterus is a fairly noisy place: there is placental noise, the mother's digestive noise, heartbeats, and breathing noise.

The mean level of the background noise in the uterus is estimated to be 28 dB sound pressure level (SPL). dB SPL is different from the decibel A filter or dBA, but for simplicity here we can treat them as the same. This sound level is similar to that in a library or while someone is whispering.

A background noise of this level is unlikely to mask a wide range of external noises. It has been estimated that external voices emitted near the mother are attenuated only by 2–3 dB. Higher speech frequencies are attenuated more than lower ones. Normal conversation spoken over 60 dB near the mother is well-transmitted in utero. See appendix for a list of common sounds quantified by loudness.

In contrast to the slightly attenuated external sounds, the maternal voice is amplified by 5-dB. This saliency may partly explain why the maternal voice is particularly loved by the infant.

It has been shown that adults can readily perceive suprasegmental features such as intonation contours of a pregnant woman's speech that have been recorded in utero and can identify about 30% of its individual phonemes. Furthermore, a recording made in utero while Beethoven's Fifth Symphony is played outside of the womb can also be correctly identified by adult listeners.

Thus, there are readily detectable sounds in the womb. So the next question becomes can the fetus hear while in the womb? If so, from what week onward can the fetus hear?

3. When can the fetus hear?

Every man is some months older than he bethinks him, for we live, move, have being…in…the womb of our mother.

— Thomas Browne (1642)

Here is a list of time points as early as which several fetal behaviors occur:

- *5–6 weeks of gestation*: Fetal heart activity

- *8–9 weeks*: General movement

- *9–10 weeks*: Isolated arm and leg movement

- *10–11 weeks*: Stretch, rotation, jaw opening, and breathing movement

- *12–14 weeks*: Sucking and swallowing

- *16 weeks*: Slow eye movements; facial expression response to sound

- *23 weeks*: Fast eye movements

- *24–25 weeks*: Cardiac, motor and brain stem response to sound

In a 2015 study, Marisa López-Teijón at Institut Marquès, Barcelona, Spain used 3D/4D ultrasound to investigate fetuses' response to intravaginally emitted music. She found that fetuses at 16 weeks of gestational age already displayed mouthing and tongue expulsion in response to the music. This suggests that the fetuses can somehow hear the music. The frequency of the tongue expulsion increases with gestational age, which is consistent with developmental trajectory. Similarly, in a 2016 study, using a two-dimensional ultrasonography, Pier F. Ferrari at the University of Parma, Italy reported that at 25 weeks' gestational age, fetuses increased their mouth openings when their mothers sang the syllable LA in a nursery rhyme.

In contrast to the facial expression response, cardiac, motor and brain stem response to sound occur around 24–25 weeks' gestation. Auditory stimuli above 105 dB elicit cardiac and motor responses as early as 24 weeks of gestation in some fetuses; they are consistently evoked in all fetuses that have been studied at 28 weeks. Brain stem connects the brain with the spinal cord and controls the communication between the motor and sensory system of the brain and the rest of the body. Sounds elicit electrical activities in the brain stem and this has been used for hearing screening. At 25 weeks, brain stem responses to sounds are consistent and reproducible in fetuses, but with very high thresholds. Nevertheless, the threshold gradually decreases with development and by 35 weeks, is just 10–20 dB higher than an adult's threshold.

Other studies have identified more mature fetal auditory responses. For instance, at 36 weeks' gestation, fetuses display a reduction in motor activity and heart rate within 10 seconds of when their mother speaks or reads aloud. This response is considered an orienting response: it indicates that the fetus is paying attention. At 36–39 weeks, fetuses can also discriminate the low-pitched piano notes D4 from C5. They show a transient decrease in heart rate when hearing C5, and when the note changes to D4, they respond with another decrease in heart rate, suggesting that they have noticed the change.

Thus, the fetus is able to hear as early as 16 weeks of gestation, which becomes more and more mature thereafter. However, given that there are detectable sounds in the womb, the question remains: does the fetus possess the ability to learn? If so, at what week does the fetus begin to learn?

4. The intelligent fetus: getting "bored" with a repeated sound

Yes. The history of man for the nine months preceding his birth would, probably, be far more interesting and contain events of greater moment than all the three score and ten years that follow it.

— Samuel Taylor Coleridge (1802)

The simplest form of learning is habituation. That is, we get used to repeated stimuli. Our reactions in terms of heart rate and body movement to the same stimulus decreases. Habituation is the ability to recognize and ignore harmless repeated stimuli. It is considered essential for normal brain functioning and requires an intact central nervous system.

A little child gets easily bored with a toy because of habituation and wanders off to find a new, unusual object. We become less surprised at the repeated blare of a car horn. Habituation is different from fatigue in that when a novel stimulus is presented, the response is recovered. When the little child finds a new, unusual toy, he becomes excited again. Even after getting used to the sound of a car horn, we may still be surprised by a sudden thunder.

Fetuses also habituate. One of the earliest studies of this was reported in 1925. In this study, a decrease in the fetal movement was observed after repeated stimulation with a car horn: a typical habituation phenomenon. In subsequent studies, similar fetal habituation (a decrease in heart rate and body movement) was reported in response to repeated sounds produced by a metal stick, the smacking of boards, and an electric toothbrush. The earliest response of fetal habituation has been observed in 22-week-old fetuses, suggesting that at as early as this, fetuses possess the ability to learn auditory stimuli.

Dutch scientist Jan G. Nijhuis, Cathelijne F. van Heteren and their colleagues have used repeated vibroacoustic stimulation to study fetal habituation. They applied a series of repeated vibratory sounds to the abdomen of pregnant women and assessed the response of their fetuses to the same stimulation 10 minutes and 24 hours later. In this study, a general movement of the fetus's trunk within one second of application of the stimulus was defined as a positive response. Lack of a positive response to four consecutive stimuli was defined as habituation. After the initial stimulus, the fetuses at 30 weeks' gestation displayed habituation 10 minutes as well as 24 hours later. It suggests that fetuses have a short-term memory of at least 10 minutes and a long-term memory of at least 24 hours. Furthermore, fetuses at 34 weeks have been found to have a long-term memory of at least four weeks: they can "remember" repeated stimuli for at least four weeks.

This finding is in line with the notion that neurocognitive functioning matures along development. Indeed, fetal habituation has been associated with functional brain development, such that older fetuses show faster habituation than younger fetuses and that well-developed fetuses exhibit faster habituation than less developed fetuses.

Research also shows that fetuses with the high proficiency of habituation exhibit advanced intellectual and mental development after birth at 6 months as well as one year of age. In contrast, fetuses with Down syndrome—a condition due to a full or partial extra copy of chromosome 21 and is associated with intellectual disability and a variety of other birth detects—take longer to habituate than normal fetuses, whereas fetuses with an encephalocele—a neural tube defect involving the incomplete closing of the brain—fail to show habituation at all.

Therefore, the fetus can learn as early as 22 weeks, at least in the simplest form and not necessarily consciously. This has been known as fetal or in utero learning.

5. The fetus can learn children's rhymes and stories

In utero learning is the new frontier.

— Norman Krasnegor (1984)

Actually, the fetus can learn not only meaningless sounds but also simple melodies and stories.

In a study by psychologist Anthony J. DeCasper, during the 33–37th week of gestation, pregnant women were asked to recite a short child's rhyme aloud each day to their fetus. At 38th week, when stimulated with a tape recording of the cited rhyme, their fetus showed a decrease in heart rate. This reduced heart rate is an example of habituation, and is interpreted as an orienting response, or that the fetus is paying attention to or becoming calmed by the familiar rhyme. Consistent with this interpretation, they show a reduced heart rate when their mother is speaking. The decrease in heart rate was absent when they were stimulated with a tape recording of a novel rhyme, although both recordings were made by an unfamiliar female voice. This suggests that the fetuses have grown familiar with the rhyme.

In another study, DeCasper further found that the fetus can maintain this memory after birth. Using the non-nutritive sucking paradigm, DeCasper found that newborn infants suck so as to hear a story that their mother has recited throughout the last six weeks of pregnancy. Here, the pregnant women were instructed to read a story in a children's book *The Cat in the Hat* aloud twice a day in a quiet place when they felt their baby was awake. Reading the story takes about three minutes; after birth, their two-day-old newborns were tested with the non-nutritive sucking paradigm. It was found that they sucked in a way to hear a recording of the recited story rather than a different novel story. The result remained the same whether the recordings were made by their mother or another stranger female. It suggests that the fetuses learned the story in utero and that the story became rewarding to them: they preferred it to others and would suck hard in order to hear it.

The earlier findings that newborns tend to suck so as to hear their own mother's voice and recordings of their native language together support the idea that fetuses possess the ability to learn in utero. This provides a neuropsychological mechanism by which their prenatal experience shapes postnatal knowledge and preferences.

This also provides an exciting opportunity for expecting parents to educate their unborn baby. But does this kind of prenatal education actually work?

PART 2: EDUCATING YOUR BABY IN THE WOMB: DOES IT WORK?

6. The four approaches to prenatal education

A caregiver who is having fun by "playing" the natural instruments of her voice, face, head, and body and orchestrating them for, and in conjunction with, her baby will be affectively "alive."

— Daniel N. Stern, *The First Relationship* (1977)

The fetus has the ability to hear as early as 16 weeks' gestation and learn from as early as 22 weeks' gestation. Their prenatal exposure creates long-lasting memory traces which persist until birth. Thus, it is tempting to conclude that prenatal education of the fetus promotes its brain development.

To find out whether or not this conclusion is true, I performed a systematic review of English and Chinese scientific literature. The inclusion criterion of this review was research conducted using any stimulation to the fetus with the intention to promote its brain, intellectual, emotional, and social development.

As a result, I found seventeen experimental and three observational studies published before July 2017. They were conducted by sixteen research teams in seven countries. These studies can be categorized into four approaches of prenatal education:

1. Playing music

2. Reading, talking, singing, and patting the mother's abdomen (sometimes combined with music)

3. Comprehensive taijiao, the traditional Chinese approach combining 1) and 2) with nutritional and psychological instruction

4. Olfactory stimulation (which would relate to food education)

In summary, the conclusion of this review is this:

When appropriately implemented, prenatal education is beneficial: it promotes the development of the fetus, especially in domains related to language and auditory processing. Benefits in motor skills and general cognitive ability has also been reported. As for food education, what the mother eats during pregnancy affects the baby's food preference in the first years of life.

7. Prenatal music

Music was my first love, it will be my last, music of the future, music of the past.

— John Miles, *Music was my first love* (1987)

The first approach to educating the fetus is prenatal music stimulation. In children and adults, listening to certain kinds of music (for instance, classical music; see Chapter 12) enhances cognitive ability and boosts mood. This observation suggests the possibility that music may also stimulate the fetuses' developing brain. To date, three research groups have tested this theory.

The first report came from Donald J. Shetler, a professor of music at the University of Rochester in 1985. He observed that babies of mothers who took private lessons of instrument music were able to imitate sounds made by adults more accurately and developed structured vocalization earlier than normal babies. They were also more attentive. Shetler then set up the "Eastman Project" to investigate whether deliberate stimulation of fetuses brings this kind of benefit. He gathered 30 pregnant women and asked them to play music to their fetus for 5–10 minutes twice a day, once a stimulative piece and then a sedative piece. In 1989, Shetler reported that music stimulated fetuses possessed more advanced language ability after birth than normal non-stimulated infants. They had more organized and articulate speech.

The second investigation was the "Firstart" program organized by the musical couple Manuel Alonso and Rosa Plaza in Spain. They studied 172 pregnant women and asked 101 of them to play a series of eight tapes of violin sounds to their fetus. On average, the mothers played music for about 50 minutes a day from 28 weeks to delivery. They were also encouraged to talk and sing to their unborn baby. In contrast, the other 71 pregnant mothers did not receive any instruction. According to two reports published in 1997 and 2001, throughout the first year, stimulated infants exhibited more advanced development in linguistic, somatosensory, motor, and cognitive domains.

The third investigation was reported in 2012 by Ravindra Arya at Cincinnati Children's Hospital Medical Centre in the U.S. Starting from 20 weeks' gestation, whereas 134 pregnant women were given standard care, only 126 pregnant women listened daily to one hour of a pre-recorded music cassette in addition to standard care. The music was a melody of instrumental music, natural sounds, and chants from religious scriptures. After birth, infants of mothers exposed to music showed superior development, including better attention and habituation to auditory and visual stimuli, and richer behavioral states indicating higher mental functions.

It seems that daily music simulation produces many favorable outcomes to the fetus. Especially in the domain of language and auditory processing it has many benefits. These benefits extend to the general cognitive domain, which is exciting.

8. Reading, talking, singing, and patting

Thinking about your fetus, talking to it, having your spouse talk to it, will all help prepare you for this new creature that's going to jump into your life and turn it upside down.

— William P. Fifer (1998)

The second approach, reading, talking, singing, and patting the mother's abdomen is another direct way of educating the fetus. Parents often read or recite children's stories and language books, and sing children's rhymes to their unborn baby while patting the mother's abdomen. Six experimental and two observational investigations studied this approach.

The six experimental investigation were conducted by:

- 1986, 1988: Rene Van de Carr, a private obstetrical practice of Hayward, California, U.S.

- 1993, 1999: Chairat Panthuraamphorn, Hua Chiew Hospital in Bangkok, Thailand

- 1993: Xunxian Cai, Shenzhen Maternity & Child Healthcare Hospital, China

- 1994: Daguang Chen, Fujian Medical School, China

In these studies, pregnant women were asked to read, talk, sing to, and/or pat on their fetus daily for 2–7 months during pregnancy. The details of the stimulations differed in each study, such that each stimulation (namely reading vs talking vs singing vs patting) lasted 5–10 minutes a day each, or all of them together lasted 5–10 minutes a day. Furthermore, patting was accompanied by music in one study. Despite these methodological differences, all studies reported positive outcomes in the infant:

- *After birth*: Faster auditory development, greater height and head circumference (indicating a more powerful brain), and able to smile and laugh at an earlier age

- *At 1.5–3 months of age*: Higher IQ scores and motor skills, including both gross (coordination of arms, legs, and movement) and fine (coordination of hands, fingers with eyes)

- *At 4 months of age*: More advanced language ability and physical growth

- *At 5 and 12 months of age*: More advanced motor skills such as sitting, staying, and walking

As an example, in the 1993 study by Chairat Panthuraamphorn, the stimulated infants turned heads to their mother's voice at 4.6 days on average after birth, while normal infants needed 3.2 months to show this reaction. This indicates prenatal stimulation robustly boosts auditory development.

Besides, one observational study was reported in 2014 by Haifeng Li at Zhejiang University, China. Li asked parents of healthy children and children with autism to retrospectively report their practice with regards to prenatal education. Parents of healthy children started fetal stimulation using language, touch, music and lighting earlier than parents of children with autism. More of them started fetal stimulation within the first three months of pregnancy. Another observational study reported in 2017 by Giuseppina Persico at the University of Milano Bicocca, Italy. Persico found that infants whose mothers sang to them were less likely to cry and wake up at night the first and second month.

These results suggest that prenatal education in the form of reading, talking, singing, and patting has extensive benefits in language and motor skills, general cognitive ability, and overall growth. It also promotes the emotional development (calming) of the fetus.

9. Comprehensive taijiao

The effect of ten years of education after birth are less than those of the ten months during pregnancy.

— Sajudang Lee, *Taegyo Singi* (*New Guidelines for Prenatal Care*, 1801)

Taijiao has been part of Chinese obstetrical culture since the Han Dynasty over two thousand years ago. "Tai" refers to fetus and "jiao" to teach, so the direct translation of taijiao is fetal education. In Korean, it is pronounced as "taegyo" and in Japanese "taikyo." A comprehensive taijiao consists of three domains:

- *Preventive domain*: Avoiding noxious and toxic foods, unpleasant scenes, unlovely sounds, and avoiding graceless sitting, standing, and sleeping postures as these may negatively affect the fetus

- *Indirect domain*: Improving nutrition and living environment, engaging in physical exercise, getting enough sleep nightly, and promoting mental health as these indirectly stimulate the fetus

- *Direct domain*: Talking, singing, reciting poetry, patting/touching mother's belly area, and listening to pleasurable music as these directly stimulate the fetus

In practice, a comprehensive taijiao program usually includes lifestyle and psychological instructions (such as those described in *The Seed of Intelligence* and *Psychology for Pregnancy*) and direct stimulation to the fetus. To date, four studies examining the effect of comprehensive taijiao on fetal development have been published in scientific journals in China. There are several studies conducted in South Korea, but all reported the finding that taijiao promoted the mother's mental health and enhanced the mother-infant bond (which we will discuss in Chapter 13), without studying its direct effect on the fetus. The four Chinese studies were conducted by:

- 2001: Yanlin Lü, People's Hospital of Zhaotong Prefecture, Yunnan Province

- 2002: Zhengai Xiong, Chongqing Medical University, Sichuan Province

- 2004: Fengjun Zhao, Liaocheng People's Hospital, Shandong Province

- 2010: Donghui Su, Jilin University, Jilin Province

These studies show that a comprehensive taijiao intervention during pregnancy produces many positive outcomes, including:

- *At birth*: More regular delivery, less premature labor, greater maternal willingness to breastfeed, and higher infant birth weight

- *Between birth and 1 month*: Playing the prenatal music significantly soothes the crying infant

- *At 6 and 12 months of age*: Advanced neurobehavioral development

- *At 30 months of age*: Advanced language and motor development including standing and walking

In addition, one study reported in 1993 by Beatriz Manrique in Venezuela investigated the effect of music stimulation combined with nutritional instruction, which is in line with the concept of taijiao. This study had by far the greatest number of subjects, 684 pregnant women. Starting from the 20th week of gestation, half of the pregnant women were given weekly 2-hour lectures on nutrition and music stimulation. Throughout the first six years, the stimulated infants showed consistently superior visual, auditory, language, memory, and motor skills over the unstimulated control infants. In addition, their mothers had greater confidence and were more active in labor, had greater success in breastfeeding, and developed a more intense bond with their infant as well as stronger family cohesion.

In summary, a comprehensive taijiao brings many benefits to the fetus. As we have discussed in the first two volumes of this series, a healthy lifestyle including a nutritious, safe diet and an optimal psychological state promote the pregnant mother's health and nourish the fetus's developing brain. Thus, it is no surprise that a comprehensive taijiao intervention has the above benefits as well. Actually, a comprehensive taijiao is always preferred to isolated direct stimulation to the fetus. An enriched physiological environment including sufficient nutrients, high levels of neurotrophic factors, and low levels of stress hormones and inflammation is the seed of full intellectual, emotional, and social development. It is the basis of any kind of learning.

10. The first food lesson

The things desired by the mother are often found
impressed on the child that the mother carries.

— Leonardo Da Vinci

During pregnancy, flavors from the mother's diet are transmitted to the amniotic fluid and swallowed by the fetus. So the fetus may learn smells and tastes from their mother's diet. At 2–4 days after birth, when given amniotic fluids from their mother and another woman to smell, they prefer their mother's, suggesting they have specific memory of their mother's odor. Fetuses show sucking and swallowing behavior at 12–14 weeks' gestation, long before they possess the ability to learn (recall that fetuses show habituation—the simplest form of learning—as early as 22 weeks).

To date, two studies have attempted to "educate" the fetus with food flavors in the assumption that prenatal exposure to certain flavors may enhance the fetus's postnatal preference towards those flavors.

The first study was conducted in 2000 by French scientist Benoist Schaal. In the last two weeks before the expected term, half of the pregnant women were asked to eat anise flavored sweets, cookies, and syrup without changing their overall food intake. Anise, sometimes called aniseed, is an herb often used as a spice. It has a unique flavor and many newborn infants dislike it: they lower their brows, raise their cheeks, wrinkle noses, close eyes, and turn heads when exposed to anise odor. Interestingly, as discovered by Schaal, newborn infants whose mothers consumed anise flavored food during pregnancy showed more tongue protruding and licking in response to anise, suggesting they liked the odor.

The second study was conducted in 2001 by American scientist Julie A. Mennella. One group of pregnant women drank carrot juice regularly during the last trimester of pregnancy. A second group drank it during the first two months of lactation. A third group never drank it. When later fed cereal prepared with carrot juice, infants of mothers who drank carrot juice during either pregnancy or lactation showed fewer negative facial expressions and enjoyed it more over the ones that had not drank any.

Thus, prenatal—as well as early postnatal—exposure to certain food flavors affects the fetus's postnatal preference towards those flavors. This is consistent with another line of evidence. First, as shown by the Avon Longitudinal Study of Parents and Children involving over 14,500 pregnancies in the Bristol area of U.K., children whose mothers consumed more fruits and vegetables during pregnancy were more likely to eat fruits and vegetables at 2–4 years of age. Second, as shown by animal experiments, a maternal high-fat diet during pregnancy enhances the offspring's preferences for diets with high-fat content. Maternal consumption of foods alters the flavor of her amniotic fluid, which changes the flavor preferences of her fetus.

Pregnancy indeed is a good "teaching moment" and a mother's healthy diet helps her unborn infant establish the life-long habit of a healthy diet.

11. How does prenatal education work?

All the distinct behaviors that make us uniquely ourselves—are, in part, also the product of conditioned learning. And the womb is where this special kind of learning begins.

— Thomas Verny, *The Secret Life of the Unborn Child* (1981)

The psychological and nutritional status of the pregnant mother is the environment of the fetus. An enriched environment promotes whereas an impoverished environment restrains your baby's developing brain. Thus, the preventive and indirect domains of taijiao benefit the fetus. We have addressed this topic in *Psychology for Pregnancy* and *The Seed of Intelligence*. Here, we look at six mechanisms by which direct prenatal stimulation promotes fetal and postnatal development.

First, as we have seen earlier, the fetus can learn and store prenatal stimuli in their memory. This memory helps them learn new information more efficiently after birth. According to a 2013 study conducted by Eino Partanen at the University of Helsinki, Finland, prenatal exposure to language enhances infants' perception of language after birth.

In this study, pregnant women were asked to play a CD containing two four-minute sequences of variants of "tatata" pseudowords to their fetus. Starting from 29 weeks of gestation throughout pregnancy, the mothers played the CD 5–7 times a week. After birth, their newborn infants were presented variants of the pseudowords while monitored by an electroencephalogram (EEG). EEG measures electrical activity of the brain and captures event-related electrical potentials. Here, the event was the trained pseudowords. It was found that these infants responded to pitch changes for the trained pseudowords with enhanced brain activity (mismatch responses, MMR). The intensity of MMR was associated with the amount of prenatal exposure such that the more their mother played the pseudowords, the more enhanced MMR the fetuses displayed in response to the pitch change. In contrast, infants with no exposure to these pseudowords before birth did not show this pattern of brain activity.

This MMR represents neural discrimination ability, which is essential for accurate speech perception. At one year of age, healthy infants show this MMR for their native language whereas very premature infants do not. This MMR further corresponds with their language performance at two years of age such that those with higher MMR possess better language ability. In the course of learning a foreign language, children and adults display enhanced MMR for changes in the speech sounds of the language. Therefore, the above finding suggests that prenatal exposure improves neural representation or sensitivity to speech, which makes the infants better learners.

Second, during pregnancy and the first few years of life, infants form an enormous number of neurons and synapses. Synapses are the connections between neurons, which are the neural substrate for learning and memory. Unless they are stimulated and used, most of these neurons and synapses will die. During this critical period, an optimal level of auditory and tactile stimulation forms an enriched environment and activates neurons and synapses. It has estimated that rat pups whose mothers were exposed to 65 dB of comfortable music during pregnancy had 30% increased neurogenesis (production of neurons) in the motor cortex, 40% increased neurogenesis in the somatosensory cortex, ncreased neurogenesis in the hippocampal critical for memory and spatial navigation). stimulation thus promotes fetal brain development.

Third, melodies and music can relax the fetus and buffer it from any potential negative stressors. Furthermore, fetuses who have been sung to during pregnancy are reported to be more calm after birth. Low levels of stress and high levels of emotional wellbeing are associated with optimal brain functioning and intellectual development (see *Fitness Powered Brains* and *Plato's Insight* for more discussion).

Fourth, melodies and music relax the pregnant mother and increase maternal arterial oxygen saturation and blood flow to the placenta. This increases blood and nutrient supply to the fetus, especially to the fetal brain. As we have discussed in *Psychology for Pregnancy*, melodies and music reduce the mother's stress levels and inflammation, the latter of which is detrimental to optimal fetal development.

Fifth, talking, reading, singing to and patting on the fetus enhance maternal-fetal bond, which promotes the mother's healthy behaviors and improves parenting quality (see Chapter 13).

Sixth, after birth, prenatal music and songs can calm crying infants and help them fall asleep and adapt in the first few months of life. Music soothes infants, but the most effective music is that which has been played to them before birth. When newborns cry, playing recordings of a maternal lullaby or prenatal music which the mother sang or played to them during pregnancy soothes the newborns and results in more down time. Rhythmic patting has a similar effect. As shown by Chairat Panthuraamphorn at the Hua Chiew Hospital in Bangkok, Thailand, when crying, rhythmic patting could calm down those infants who had been patted daily during pregnancy in 2.1 minutes, while it took the unpatted infants twice as long to settle. Prenatal education thus provides a powerful caregiving tool for the parents. Singing lullabies during pregnancy also makes the mothers more confident and develop a greater ability to sing to and care for their infant after delivery.

PART 3: PRACTICE: A FURTHER LOOK AT PRENATAL EDUCATION

12. What music: the Mozart effect

The importance of unconscious listening to music is not less than that of listening to a language.

— Edwin Gordon, *Primary Measures of Music Audiation* (1979)

In 1993, three scientists Frances H. Rauscher, Gordon L. Shaw, Katherine N. Ky at the University of California, Irvine published a classic study in the journal *Nature*. They reported the surprising observation that, after listening to 10 minutes of Mozart's pleasant, energetic Sonata in D Major (K448), college students showed substantially better spatial-temporal reasoning skills than after listening to relaxation instructions or silence before taking the tests. Spatial-temporal reasoning skills involve manipulating images of things in space and time to solve multi-step problems. It is essential for high-level brain functions that people use to play chess and do math, science, and other complex tasks. When translated to spatial IQ scores, listening to Mozart led to a boost of 8–9 points. Although the benefit lasted only 10–15 minutes, it has since then become known as the "Mozart effect."

In a follow-up study, the three scientists confirmed that the benefit in spatial-temporal reasoning abilities gains just from listening to Mozart rather than a minimalist work by Philip Glass or a dance piece (trance music). Since then, dozens of experiments have confirmed the Mozart effect. One 2010 meta-analysis of 39 experiments reported consistent advantage in spatial-temporal abilities after listening to Mozart's Sonata (K. 448) compared to listening to a nonmusical stimulus or sitting in silence. Nevertheless, scientists also found that the benefit holds true for other pieces of Mozart and other classical music whether or not it was composed by Mozart. Therefore, there also exists a Schubert effect for example. Sad sounding classical music such as Albinoni's Adagio does not seem to have the benefit.

One special feature of Mozart's music is its complex melodic variations. Compared to simpler music, this may provide greater stimulation to the prefrontal cortex, the CEO of our brain. Indeed, in functional neuroimaging research, Mozart's Sonata (K. 448) has been found to activate the auditory as well as the prefrontal cortex. In EEG research, it enhances synchrony of the firing pattern of the right frontal and left temporoparietal areas of the brain. In rats, listening to Mozart's Sonata (K. 448) throughout pregnancy plus two months after birth has been found to enhance maze learning (completing the maze rapidly and with few errors) in young adulthood compared to listening to a minimalist music (a Philip Glass composition), white noise, or silence. In preterm human infants, listening to Mozart lowers resting energy expenditure, improves weight gain, and attenuates pain response from heel lance.

On the other hand, it is also believed that Mozart's music is simply one example of stimuli that promote positive feelings and arousal levels. For instance, watching a comedy excerpt or engaging in brief physical exercise (such as cycling or playing tennis, read *Fitness Powered Brains* for more information about this topic) also enhances cognitive performance. In this regard, any pleasurable music will benefit both you and your fetus.

Pleasurable music can be categorized into stimulative (arousing) and sedative in terms of its effect on mood. Stimulative music is characterized by a fast tempo (such as 70-90 beats per minute), an irregular or syncopated rhythm, and wide jumps between notes of the melody line. It stimulates the listeners, making them energetic. Mozart's Sonata (K. 448) is a typical example. Sedative music is characterized by a slow tempo (such as 60–72 beats per minute), a regular and steady rhythm, and minimal jumps between notes of the melody line. It relaxes and calms the listener. Lullabies and children's music are often sedative. Typical examples that have been used in research and were found to calm infants include:

- *Barney Song (I Love You)*

- *Brahm's Lullaby*

- *Itsy Bitsy Spider*

- *Jesus Loves Me*

- *Rock-a-Bay Baby*

- *Twinkle, Twinkle, Little Star*

- And many traditional Chinese, German, and Iranian lullabies

Besides listening to music, you may play music yourself. Playing music promotes your mental health and cognitive abilities, which will prepare you for parenting.

13. LoveStart: sing to your baby, even if you are a bad singer

It seems to me that one has not had all his rights if he has not floated into consciousness to the sound of his mother's voice, singing.

— May Lamberton Becker, *First Adventures in Reading: Introducing Children to Books* (1936)

According to a 2009 study, infants clearly prefer the unaccompanied to accompanied version of an unfamiliar song. Unaccompanied version means voice only, while accompanied version means voice with instrumental accompaniment. When 5, 8 and 11-month old Canadian infants were played the two versions of a Chinese song (sung by a 9-year-old girl), all listened to the unaccompanied version longer, indicating infants prefer the pure, simple human voice.

This is good news for parents. Although parents who have music education or singing experiences are more likely to sing to their infants, you don't need a music degree to serenade your baby. What matters is that you sing, not that you sing well. Recall that the fetus's and infant's favorite sound is their mother's voice—they do listen to it every day.

On one hand, singing is an auditory stimulation to the fetus, which constitutes an enriched environment and boosts the fetus's developing brain. On the other hand, singing promotes a caring relationship known as the mother-infant bond or attachment.

Mother-infant bond is an interaction between a mother and her baby. During pregnancy, mother-infant bond refers to the affective valence of maternal love towards the fetus. It is indicated by a pregnant woman stroking her abdomen, singing and talking to her child, and imagining the sex and appearance of the unborn child.

Higher levels of mother-infant bond are associated with healthier maternal behaviors. Mothers with a high level of mother-infant bond are more likely to seek out prenatal care, consume a nutritious diet, engage in regular physical exercise, and have better overall psychological health. Mother-infant bond is also rather stable as it persists after birth, and is responsible for the initiation of sensitive parenting behavior. Thus, high levels of mother-infant bond have been linked to a more secure infant temperament, better cognitive development, greater ability to socialize with peers, and more coherent family dynamics. In fact, many scholars believe that the core of prenatal education is to boost this caring relationship.

Singing to the fetus is particularly important, because it is characterized by high emotional engagement. It has been estimated that around 70% of parents sing to their (unborn) baby regularly. Parental, and particularly maternal, singing is characterized by a high pitch, slow tempo, and high emotional engagement. Singing to the fetus is an emotional expression of love and enhances mother-infant bond.

14. Talk and read to your baby: the start of a favorable home literacy environment

Language is one of the most powerful symbolic systems through which children learn to understand and interpret their physical, social, and conceptual worlds.

— Susan M. Sheridan et al. (2011)

As a direct stimulation to the fetus, many parents talk and read children's stories to their baby during pregnancy. The fetus can store these stories in their memory and become better language learners after birth.

This prenatal education is crucial since early language learning ability is the basis for success at school. The higher the ability to read and write, to recognize vocabularies, and to comprehend stories, the higher the academic achievement. Neurobiological research indicates that from pregnancy through the first three years after birth, the infant acquires language in a bottom-up way. They extract basic segmental and suprasegmental features of speech through listening. This is primarily implemented in the temporal cortex. From the fourth year continuing into adolescence, a top-down way of active analysis of syntactic relations his is implemented in the inferior frontal cortex, is highlights the importance of a favorable early e literacy environment.

A favorable early home literacy environment is characterized by more frequent parental reading, early talking and reading to the child, a variety of books owned at home, and frequent library visits. Early home literacy is critical because this is the context in which children first acquire language and literacy skills. The latter allows them to make sense of and interact with the world. Comparing the parenting difference—primarily studied after birth—between families at high and low socioeconomic status (SES) provides an excellent example.

High-SES parents (for instance, those who are doctors or lawyers) prepare their child for life early. They cultivate their child's abilities for questioning and analytic minds from a young age. They talk to their child often, with commentary about the surrounding world, about their own experiences, emotions, and ideas. They question the child on his needs and interests. They involve their child in dinner conversations, exposing the child to various vocabulary, information, and analytic thinking. They have more books and read books often to their child starting at an early age. When reading, they try to elaborate on what is read in the book, make connections and explanations in the story, and relate it to the real world. They also encourage their child to talk and think about the story by asking them questions.

In contrast, low-SES parents (for instance, those whose incomes fall below the poverty line) talk less to their child. When they talk, it is usually in the form of commands and orders with little cognitive involvement of the child. They carry on discussions at the dinner table with the assumption that the child has nothing to do with it or no interest in participating. They have limited books at home and only sometimes read to their child. However, during reading, they seldom explain what is being read, or connect it to the real world.

It is estimated that during interactions with their child, high-SES parents speak about 2000 words per hour. Low-SES parents speak only about 1300. By the age of three, the child in a high-SES family has heard about 30 million words, compared to 20 million by their peers raised in low-SES families. Given this difference, their offspring show robustly different cognitive developments. Several well-designed adoption studies conducted in the United States and Europe found that children raised in high-SES families possess IQs that are on average 12–18 points higher than those children raised in a low-SES family. Clearly, high-SES parents create a more favorable home literacy environment for their child, which in turn boosts their child's developing brain.

Reading is as important as talking, since books contain more complex and advanced vocabulary than everyday conversations. In a 2016 study by Frank Niklas at the University of Melbourne, Australia, about half of the children were read to before they were 6 months old. Interestingly, the earlier a child was read to the greater his rhyming, verbal comprehension and reasoning abilities were in kindergarten.

15. A double-edged sword: the risk of overstimulation

Guo you bu ji [Going too far is as bad as not enough].

— Chinese Proverb

Given the above-reviewed studies, prenatal stimulation boosts the fetus's developing brain. However, there also exists a serious concern about the safety of the stimulation. Overstimulation may disrupt normal brain functioning in fetuses and infants.

A series of experiments conducted by Robert Lickliter at Virginia Polytechnic Institute and State University in the 1990s provided robust evidence. Bobwhite quail chicks were exposed to 10 or 40 minutes per hour of patterned auditory stimulation (bobwhite contentment calls) or visual lighting during the last day prior to hatching. On the days following hatching, those exposed to 10 minutes of stimulation exhibited an accelerated development of species-typical perceptual responsiveness. In contrast, those exposed to 40 minutes of stimulation exhibited abnormal species-typical perceptual responsiveness. They showed deficits in both auditory and visual responsiveness and had higher rates of mortality, suggesting there exists a threshold of sensory stimulation surpassing which negative consequences occur.

Thus, it has been reported that in fetal sheep, exposure to a 120 dB broadband noise—slightly noisier than a rock band—for 16 hours damaged hair cells, which are sensory receptors in the ear. In rat pups, compared to those born to mothers raised in a normal, quiet environment, those whose mothers were exposed to 95 dB of sound—loudness equivalent to a farm tractor or garbage truck—an hour a day during pregnancy had 11.5% decreased neurogenesis (production of neurons) in the somatosensory cortex. They also had 30% decreased neurogenesis in the motor cortex, 50% reduced neurogenesis in the hippocampal dentate gyrus area and 30% reduced neurogenesis in the hippocampal CA1 area. This suggests that overstimulation causes deficits not only in the sensory-related brain areas but also in motor and memory-related areas.

In humans, it has been estimated that fetuses that are exposed to intermittent noise at above 80 dB—the noise level of average city traffic—from television, boomboxes, or machinery show two months of delayed language development at 40 weeks' gestation. At birth, noise-exposed fetuses possess a smaller head circumference indicating a smaller, less effective brain. Furthermore, children of mothers who worked in a noisy environment (85–95 dBA) during pregnancy are three-fold more at risk for hearing loss.

One important way by which noise causes broad damage to the brain is by interfering with sleep. Just like a newborn, the fetus sleeps the vast majority of the day. Sleep plays a pivotal role in brain development and sleep deprivation inhibits the production of neurons and synapses.

Since the discovery of the benefits of fetal stimulation programs, the industry has produced many music devices for the fetus. Some parents also directly put head phones on the mother's abdomen to play music to the fetus. However, this may not necessarily be safe. In utero, sound is nondirectional, meaning the sound from music devices or head phones directly attached to the abdomen will be additive and may produce extremely intense noise in the womb. The safest way therefore is to avoid these devices and play music openly in the environment. You can adapt and monitor the volume of music with your own ear.

Finally, there is compelling evidence that there is light in the womb and the fetus can see. We mentioned one study using lighting as a prenatal stimulation, but to date no study has clarified the conditions under which lighting stimulation achieves beneficial rather than negative consequences. Thus, at this moment, any lighting stimulation to the fetus should be used with caution.

16. The wonder of prenatal education: take home message

By creating a warm, emotionally enriching environment in utero, a woman can make a decisive difference in everything her child feels, hopes, dreams, thinks, and accomplishes throughout life. During these months, a woman is her baby's conduit to the world. Everything that affects her, affects him.

> — Thomas Verny, *The Secret Life of the Unborn Child* (1981)

From as early as 12–14 weeks' gestation, your baby can suck and swallow. From as early as 16 weeks, they can hear. From 22 weeks onward, they possess the ability to learn. What they learn in the womb affects their postnatal experience, their intellectual and emotional development. Therefore, when appropriately implemented, prenatal education provides the fetus a stimulating, enriched environment, and this very first lesson will situate the fetus in a beneficial position at the start of a life-long journey.

n the studies we reviewed above, the practices seems to be safe, pleasurable, and ng:

- Listen to pleasurable music for 20–30 minutes twice a day, when you feel your fetus is awake. You may choose to listen to a stimulative piece once and a sedative piece at another time, according to your own mood or your baby's mood.

- Talk, read/recite children's stories and language books, and sing children's rhymes (while patting perhaps) 5–10 minutes a day, when you feel your fetus is awake.

- As the fetus can hear as early as 16 weeks of gestation, start the above stimulation around this time. Considering the benefits of listening to music for your own health (see *Psychology for Pregnancy*), you may start listening to music as early as possible, preferably before pregnancy.

- Avoid noisy environments; when you play music, talk, read, or sing to your unborn baby, pay close attention to the volume. Loudness at normal conversation levels, around 60–65 dBA, is safe and well-perceived by the fetus.

- Eat healthily (see *The Seed of Intelligence*), as it not only improves your physical and psychological health but also teaches your fetus its very first food lesson on nutritional eating.

Meanwhile, keep in mind that although the fetus possesses the ability to learn, that ability is actually quite limited.

Learning is fastest when the brain is fully mature. A healthy lifestyle including a nutritious diet and enriching living environment, and an optimal psychological state are the seeds of your baby's developing brain. Therefore, sow the best seeds so your baby can bloom into a healthy, thriving adult.

APPENDIX: Common sounds quantified by loudness

- 110 dBA: Rock band, symphony orchestra

- 98 dBA: Farm tractor, garbage truck

- 88 dBA: Subway, motorcycle (Very annoying)

- 85–111 dBA: Cello

- 85–90 dBA: Food blender, lawnmower

- 84–103 dBA: Piano Fortissimo

- 82–92 dBA: Violin

- 80 dBA: Telephone dial tone, average city traffic (Annoying; interferes with conversation)

- 78 dBA: Washing machine

- 75–85 dBA: Chamber music, small auditorium

- 75 dBA: Dishwasher

- 70 dBA: Hair dryer, vacuum cleaner, Fortissimo Singer 3' (Intrusive; interferes with telephone conversation)

- 60–70 dBA: Normal piano practice

- 50–65 dBA: Normal conversation

- 50–60 dBA: Quiet office (Comfortable hearing levels are under 60 dB)

- 40 dBA: Refrigerator humming

- 30 dBA: Whisper, library

- 20–30 dBA: Bedroom at night

- 20 dBA: Rustling leaves (Just audible)

- 10 dBA: Normal breathing

REFERENCES

Quotes

Beth Skwarecki (2013, August) Babies Learn to Recognize Words in the Womb. *Science News.* Available http://www.sciencemag.org/news/2013/08/babies-learn-recognize-words-womb (final accessed 2017/08/21).

Aidan Macfarlane. (1977). *The psychology of childbirth.* Harvard University Press.

William P. Fifer… Cited in Janet L. Hopson. (Sep/Oct 1998). Fetal Psychology: Your baby can feel, dream and even listen to Mozart in the womb. Psychology Today. Available at https://www.psychologytoday.com/articles/199809/fetal-psychology (final accessed 2017/08/21).

Chang, S., Park, S., & Chung, C. (2004). Effect of Taegyo-focused prenatal education on maternal-fetal attachment and self-efficacy related to childbirth. *Journal of Korean Academy of Nursing*, 34(8), 1409-1415.

Kolata, G. (1984). Studying learning in the womb. *Science*, 225, 302-304.

Verny, T. R., Kelly, J., & Pennycook, R. (1981). *The secret life of the unborn child.* New York: Summit Books.

Brand, M. (1985). Lullabies that awaken musicality in infants. *Music Educators Journal*, 71 (7), 28-31.

1. A newborn's preference

DeCasper, A.J., and Fifer, W.P. (1980). Of human bonding: Newborns prefer their mothers' voices. *Science* 208, 1174–1176.

Moon, C., Cooper, R.P., and Fifer, W.P. (1993). Two-day-olds prefer their native language. *Infant Behav. Dev.* 16, 495–500.

Mampe, B., Friederici, A. D., Christophe, A., & Wermke, K. (2009). Newborns' cry melody is shaped by their native language. *Current biology*, *19*(23), 1994-1997.

Moon, C. M., & Fifer, W. P. (2000). Evidence of transnatal auditory learning. *Journal of Perinatology*, *20*(S8), S37.

2. Your baby's auditory world: sounds in the womb

Querleu, D., Renard, X., Boutteville, C., & Crepin, G. (1989, October). Hearing by the human fetus? In *Seminars in perinatology* (Vol. 13, No. 5, pp. 409-420).

Busnel, M. C., GRANIER-DEFERRE, C., & Lecanuet, J. P. (1992). Fetal audition. *Annals of the New York Academy of Sciences*, 662(1), 118-134.

Richards, D. S., Frentzen, B., Gerhardt, K. J., McCANN, M. E., & Abrams, R. M. (1992). Sound levels in the human uterus. *Obstetrics & Gynecology*, *80*(2), 186-190.

Abrams, R. M., Griffiths, S. K., Huang, X., Sain, J., Langford, G., & Gerhardt, K. J. (1998). Fetal music perception: The role of sound transmission. *Music Perception: An Interdisciplinary Journal*, *15*(3), 307-317.

Beth Skwarecki (2013, August) Babies Learn to Recognize Words in the Womb. *Science News*. Available http://www.sciencemag.org/news/2013/08/babies-learn-recognize-words-womb (final accessed 2017/08/21)

3. When can the fetus hear?

Nijhuis, J. G. (2003). Fetal behavior. *Neurobiology of aging*, 24, S41-S46.

Busnel, M. C., GRANIER-DEFERRE, C., & Lecanuet, J. P. (1992). Fetal audition. *Annals of the New York Academy of Sciences*, 662(1), 118-134.

Graven, S. N., & Browne, J. V. (2008). Auditory development in the fetus and infant. *Newborn and infant nursing reviews*, *8*(4), 187-193.

López-Teijón, M., García-Faura, Á., & Prats-Galino, A. (2015). Fetal facial expression in response to intravaginal music emission. *Ultrasound*, *23*(4), 216-223.

Ferrari, G. A., Nicolini, Y., Demuru, E., Tosato, C., Hussain, M., Scesa, E., & Palagi, E. (2016). Ultrasonographic investigation of human fetus responses to maternal communicative and non-communicative stimuli. *Frontiers in psychology*, 7.

Hepper, P. G., Scott, D., & Shahidullah, S. (1993). Newborn and fetal response to maternal voice. *Journal of Reproductive and Infant Psychology*, *11*(3), 147-153.

Voegtline, K. M., Costigan, K. A., Pater, H. A., and DiPietro, J. A. (2013). Nearterm fetal response to maternal spoken voice. *Infant Behav. Dev.* 36, 526–533

Lecanuet, J. P., Graniere-Deferre, C., Jacquet, A. Y., & DeCasper, A. J. (2000). Fetal discrimination of low-pitched musical notes. *Developmental psychobiology*, *36*(1), 29-39.

4. The intelligent fetus: getting "bored" with a repeated sound

Jeffrey, W. E., & Cohen, L. B. (1971). Habituation in the human infant. *Advances in child development and behavior*, 6, 63-97.

Peiper, A. (1925). Sinnesempfindungen des Kindes vor seiner Geburt. *Monatsschr Kinderheilkd*, *29*, 236.

Forbes, H. S., & Forbes, H. B. (1927). Fetal sense reaction: hearing. *Journal of Comparative Psychology*, *7*(5), 353.

Ray, W. S. (1932). A preliminary report on a study of fetal conditioning. *Child Development*, *3*(2), 175-177.

Leader, L. R., Baillie, P., Martin, B., & Vermeulen, E. (1982). The assessment and significance of habituation to a repeated stimulus by the human fetus. *Early human development*, *7*(3), 211-219.

Kuhlman, K. A., Burns, K. A., Depp, R., & Sabbagha, R. E. (1988). Ultrasonic imaging of normal fetal response to external vibratory acoustic stimulation. *American Journal of Obstetrics and Gynecology*, *158*(1), 47-51.

Groome, L. J., Gotlieb, S. J., Neely, C. L., & Waters, M. D. (1993). Developmental trends in fetal habituation to vibroacoustic stimulation. *American Journal of Perinatology*, *10*(01), 46-49.

Morokuma, S., Fukushima, K., Kawai, N., Tomonaga, M., Satoh, S., & Nakano, H. (2004). Fetal habituation correlates with functional brain development. *Behavioural brain research*, *153*(2), 459-463.

Van Heteren, C. F., Boekkooi, P. F., Jongsma, H. W., & Nijhuis, J. G. (2000). Fetal learning and memory. *The Lancet*, *356*(9236), 1169-1170.

Dirix, C. E., Nijhuis, J. G., Jongsma, H. W., & Hornstra, G. (2009). Aspects of fetal learning and memory. *Child Development*, *80*(4), 1251-1258.

Gaultney, J. F., & Gingras, J. L. (2005). Fetal rate of behavioral inhibition and preference for novelty during infancy. *Early human development*, *81*(4), 379-386.

Leader, L. R., Baillie, P., Martin, B., Molteno, C., & Wynchank, S. (1984). Fetal responses to vibrotactile stimulation, a possible predictor of fetal and neonatal outcome. *Australian and New Zealand Journal of Obstetrics and Gynaecology*, *24*(4), 251-256.

Dustman, R. E., & Callner, D. A. (1979). Cortical evoked responses and response decrement in nonretarded and Down's syndrome individuals. *American Journal of Mental Deficiency*.

Hepper, P. G., & Shahidullah, S. (1992). Habituation in normal and Down's syndrome fetuses. *Quarterly Journal of Experimental Psychology: Section B*, *44*(3-4), 305-317.

van Heteren, C. F., Boekkooi, P. F., Jongsma, H. W., & Nijhuis, J. G. (2000). Responses to vibroacoustic stimulation in a fetus with an encephalocele compared to responses of normal fetuses. *Journal of perinatal medicine*, *28*(4), 306-308.

5. The fetus can learn children's rhymes and stories

DeCasper, A. J., Lecanuet, J. P., Busnel, M. C., Granier-Deferre, C., & Maugeais, R. (1994). Fetal reactions to recurrent maternal speech. *Infant behavior and development*, *17*(2), 159-164.

DeCasper, A. J., & Spence, M. J. (1986). Prenatal maternal speech influences newborns' perception of speech sounds. *Infant behavior and Development*, 9(2), 133-150.

Partanen, E., Kujala, T., Näätänen, R., Liitola, A., Sambeth, A., & Huotilainen, M. (2013). Learning-induced neural plasticity of speech processing before birth. *Proceedings of the National Academy of Sciences*, 110(37), 15145-15150.

Cheour, M., Ceponiene, R., Lehtokoski, A., Luuk, A., Allik, J., Alho, K., & Näätänen, R. (1998). Development of language-specific phoneme representations in the infant brain. *Nature neuroscience*, *1*(5).

Jansson-Verkasalo, E., Ruusuvirta, T., Huotilainen, M., Alku, P., Kushnerenko, E., Suominen, K., ... & Hallman, M. (2010). Atypical perceptual narrowing in prematurely born infants is associated with compromised language acquisition at 2 years of age. *BMC neuroscience*, *11*(1), 88.

Winkler, I., Kujala, T., Tiitinen, H., Sivonen, P., Alku, P., Lehtokoski, A., ... & Näätänen, R. (1999). Brain responses reveal the learning of foreign language phonemes. *Psychophysiology*, *36*(5), 638-642.

Cheour, M., Korpilahti, P., Martynova, O., & Lang, A. H. (2001). Mismatch negativity and late discriminative negativity in investigating speech perception and learning in children and infants. *Audiology and Neurotology*, *6*(1), 2-11.

7. Prenatal music

Arabin, B. (2002). Music during pregnancy. *Ultrasound in Obstetrics & Gynecology*, 20(5), 425-430.

Chamberlain, D. B. (2012). Prenatal stimulation: Experimental results. *Birth Psychology*/accessed June, 20.

Cheng, F. K. (2016). Taijiao: a traditional Chinese approach to enhancing fetal growth through maternal physical and mental health. *Chinese Nursing Research*, *3*(2), 49-53.

Shetler, D. J. (1985). Prelude to a musical life: Prenatal music experiences. *Music Educators Journal*, 71 (7), 26-27.

Shetler, D. J. (1989). The inquiry into prenatal musical experience: A report of the Eastman project 1980–1987. *Journal of Prenatal & Perinatal Psychology & Health*. 3(3): 171-190

Lafuente, M. J., Grifol, R., Segarra, J., Soriano, J., Gorba, M. A., & Montesinos, A. (1997). Effects of the Firstart method of prenatal stimulation on psychomotor development: The first six months. *Pre-and Peri-Natal Psychology Journal*, *11*(3), 151.

Lafuente, M. J., Grifol, R., & Rios, D. R. (2001). Effects of the Firstart method of prenatal stimulation on psychomotor development: From six to twelve months. *Journal of Prenatal & Perinatal Psychology & Health*, *15*(3), 207.

Arya, R., Chansoria, M., Konanki, R., & Tiwari, D. K. (2012). Maternal music exposure during pregnancy influences neonatal behaviour: an open-label randomized controlled trial. *International journal of pediatrics*, *2012*.

8. Reading, talking, singing, and patting

Van de Carr, R., & Lehrer, M. (1986). Enhancing early speech, parental bonding and infant physical development using prenatal intervention in standard obstetric practice. *Journal of Prenatal & Perinatal Psychology & Health.* 1(1), 20-30.

Carr, F., & Lehrer, M. (1988). Prenatal University; commitment to fetal-family bonding and the strengthening of the family unit as an educational institution. *Pre-and Perinatal Psychology Journal*, *3*(2), 87.

Panthuraamphorn, C. (1993). Prenatal infant stimulation program. *Prenatal perception, learning, and bonding*, 187-220.

Panthuraamphorn, C., Dookchitra, D., & Sanmaneechai, M. (1999). The outcome of fetal response and learning to prenatal stimuli. *International Journal of Prenatal and Perinatal Psychology and Medicine*, *11*, 173-182.

Cai, X., Wong, K. (1993). Tai jiao dui ying er zhi neng ying xiang de yan jiu. *Chinese Journal of Birth Health & Heredity*, 3 DOI:10.13404/j.cnki.cjbhh.1993.03.012

Chen, D. G., Huang, Y. F., Zhang, J. Y., & Qi, G. P. (1994). Influence of prenatal music and touch-enrichment on the IQ, motor development, and behavior of infants. *Chinese Mental Health Journal*, *8*(8), 148-151.

Li HF, Sun AJ, Xu JL, Wang JP, Xia ZZ. Study on the relationships between foetal education and childhood autism. *J Hangzhou Normal Univ (Natural Science Edition)*. 2014;13:360e364 (in Chinese).

Persico, G., Antolini, L., Vergani, P., Costantini, W., Nardi, M. T., & Bellotti, L. (2017). Maternal singing of lullabies during pregnancy and after birth: Effects on mother–infant bonding and on newborns' behaviour. Concurrent Cohort Study. *Women and Birth*.

9. Comprehensive taijiao

Cheng, F. K. (2016). Taijiao: a traditional Chinese approach to enhancing fetal growth through maternal physical and mental health. *Chinese Nursing Research*, *3*(2), 49-53.

Chang, S., Park, S., & Chung, C. (2004). Effect of Taegyo-focused prenatal education on maternal-fetal attachment and self-efficacy related to childbirth. *Journal of Korean Academy of Nursing*, *34*(8), 1409-1415.

Lee, Y., Lee, J., & Tulo, N. B. (2016). Korean Forest Taegyo for Reducing Stress and Emotional Instability during Pregnancy. *International Journal of Childbirth Education*, *31*(4), 24.

Lv YL, Zhang CP, Ding H, Lv GM, Zhu AH. Clinical applications research of fetal teaching. *Chin J Birth Health Hered*. 2001;9(65e66):127e128 (in Chinese).

Xiong, Z., Dan, Y., Liu, X. (2002) Tai jiao yu yun qi jian ce de lin chuang ying yong yan jiu. *Chinese Journal of Primary Medicine Pharmacy* 10. (in Chinese).

Zhao, F. (2004). Shi shi tai jiao de xiao guo ping jia. *Heilongjiang Nursing Journal* 1. (in Chinese).

Su, D. (2010). Tai jiao dui xin sheng er shen jing xing wei de ying xiang. *Maternal and Child Health Care of China*, 21 (in Chinese).

Manrique, B., Contasti, M., Alvaredo, M. A., Zypman, M., Palma, N., Ierrobino, M. T., ... & Carini, D. (1993). Nurturing parents to stimulate their children from prenatal stage to three years of age. *Prenatal Perception, Learning and Bonding. Berlin: Leonardo Publishers*, 153-86.

Manrique, B., Contasti, M., Alvarado, M. A., Zypman, M., Palma, N., Ierrobino, M. T., ... & Carini, D. (1998). A controlled experiment in prenatal enrichment with 684 families in Caracas, Venezuela: Results to age six. *Journal of Prenatal & Perinatal Psychology & Health*, *12*(3/4), 209.

10. The first food lesson

Schaal, B., Marlier, L., & Soussignan, R. (1998). Olfactory function in the human fetus: evidence from selective neonatal responsiveness to the odor of amniotic fluid. *Behavioral neuroscience*, *112*(6), 1438-1449.

Marlier, L., Schaal, B., & Soussignan, R. (1998). Neonatal responsiveness to the odor of amniotic and lacteal fluids: a test of perinatal chemosensory continuity. *Child development*, *69*(3), 611-623.

Mennella, J. A., Johnson, A., & Beauchamp, G. K. (1995). Garlic ingestion by pregnant women alters the odor of amniotic fluid. *Chemical senses*, *20*(2), 207-209.

Schaal, B., Marlier, L., & Soussignan, R. (2000). Human foetuses learn odours from their pregnant mother's diet. Chemical senses, 25(6), 729-737.

Mennella, J. A., Jagnow, C. P., & Beauchamp, G. K. (2001). Prenatal and postnatal flavor learning by human infants. *Pediatrics*, *107*(6), e88-e88.

Emmett, P. M., Jones, L. R., & Golding, J. (2015). Pregnancy diet and associated outcomes in the Avon Longitudinal Study of Parents and Children. *Nutrition reviews*, *73*(suppl_3), 154-174.

Ong, Z. Y., & Muhlhausler, B. S. (2011). Maternal "junk-food" feeding of rat dams alters food choices and development of the mesolimbic reward pathway in the offspring. *The FASEB Journal*, *25*(7), 2167-2179.

11. How does prenatal education work?

Kim, H., Lee, M. H., Chang, H. K., Lee, T. H., Lee, H. H., Shin, M. C., ... & Kim, C. J. (2006). Influence of prenatal noise and music on the spatial memory and neurogenesis in the hippocampus of developing rats. *Brain and Development*, 28(2), 109-114.

Kim, C. H., Lee, S. C., Shin, J. W., Chung, K. J., Lee, S. H., Shin, M. S., ... & Kim, K. H. (2013). Exposure to music and noise during pregnancy influences neurogenesis and thickness in motor and somatosensory cortex of rat pups. *International neurourology journal*, *17*(3), 107.

Wilkin, P. E. (1995). A comparison of fetal and newborn responses to music and sound stimuli with and without daily exposure to a specific piece of music. *Bulletin of the Council for research in music education*, 163-169.

Liu, Y.B., Li, Y.C., Huang, Y.L. (2013) An evaluation of prenatal education effect foetal hemodynamic and behavioural rating by four-dimensional colour Doppler. *Mod Instr Med Treat*. 19:18e20 (in Chinese).

Ye, H., Zhou, M., Chen, Y. (2005). Tai jiao yin yue dui yun fu he tai er de ying yiang. *Maternal and Child Health Care of China*. 3 (in Chinese).

Sirak, C. (2012). *Mothers' singing to fetuses: The effect of music education*. The Florida State University.

Tabarro, C. S., Campos, L. B. D., Galli, N. O., Novo, N. F., & Pereira, V. M. (2010). Effect of the music in labor and newborn. *Revista da Escola de Enfermagem da USP*, *44*(2), 445-452.

Polverini-Rey, R. (1992). *Intrauterine musical learning: The soothing effect on newborns of a lullaby learned prenatally (Dissertation)*. Los Angeles: California School of Professional Psychology.

Montemurro, R., & Rosario, N. (1996). Singing lullabies to unborn children: Experiences in village Vilamarxant, Spain. *Journal of Prenatal & Perinatal Psychology & Health*, 11 (1), 9-16

Carolan, M., Barry, M., Gamble, M., Turner, K., & Mascarenas, O. (2011). Singing lullabies in pregnancy: What benefits for women? *Women and Birth*, 24 (Supplement 1), S29.

Busnel, M. C., GRANIER-DEFERRE, C., & Lecanuet, J. P. (1992). Fetal audition. *Annals of the New York Academy of Sciences*, *662*(1), 118-134.

Polverini-Rey, R. A. (1993). *Intrauterine musical learning: The soothing effect on newborns of a lullaby learned prenatally (Dissertation)*. Los Angeles, CA, California School of Professional Psychology.

12. What music to listen: the Mozart effect

Rauscher, F. H., Shaw, G. L., & Ky, C. N. (1993). Music and spatial task performance. *Nature*, 365(6447), 611-611.

Rauscher, F. H., Shaw, G. L., & Ky, K. N. (1995). Listening to Mozart enhances spatial-temporal reasoning: towards a neurophysiological basis. *Neuroscience letters*, 185(1), 44-47.

Pietschnig, J., Voracek, M., & Formann, A. K. (2010). Mozart effect–Shmozart effect: A meta-analysis. *Intelligence*, *38*(3), 314-323.

Hetland, L. (2000). Listening to music enhances spatial-temporal reasoning: Evidence for the" Mozart Effect". *Journal of Aesthetic Education*, *34*(3/4), 105-148.

Thompson, W. F., Schellenberg, E. G., & Husain, G. (2001). Arousal, mood, and the Mozart effect. *Psychological science*, *12*(3), 248-251.

Muftuler, L. T., Bodner, M., Shaw, G. L., & Nalcioglu, O. (1999). fMRI of Mozart effect using auditory stimuli. *Neurol Res*, *20*, 666.

Rideout, B. E., & Laubach, C. M. (1996). EEG correlates of enhanced spatial performance following exposure to music. *Perceptual and motor skills*, *82*(2), 427-432.

Schellenberg, E.G., & Weiss, M.W. (2013). Music and cognitive abilities. In D. Deutsch (Ed.), *The psychology of music*(3rd ed., pp. 499-550). Amsterdam: Elsevier.

Schellenberg, E. G. (2012). Cognitive performance after listening to music: a review of the Mozart effect. *Music, health, and wellbeing*, 324-338.

Chen, C. (2017). *Plato's Insight: How Physical Exercise Boosts Mental Excellence*. London: Brain & Life Publishing

Rauscher, F., Robinson, D., & Jens, J. (1998). Improved maze learning through early music exposure in rats. *Neurological research*, *20*(5), 427-432.

Lubetzky, R., Mimouni, F. B., Dollberg, S., Reifen, R., Ashbel, G., & Mandel, D. (2010). Effect of music by Mozart on energy expenditure in growing preterm infants. *Pediatrics*, *125*(1), e24-e28.

Cavaiuolo, C., Casani, A., Di Manso, G., & Orfeo, L. (2015). Effect of Mozart music on heel prick pain in preterm infants: a pilot randomized controlled trial. *Journal of Pediatric and Neonatal Individualized Medicine (JPNIM)*, *4*(1), e040109.

Amini, E., Rafiei, P., Zarei, K., Gohari, M., & Hamidi, M. (2013). Effect of lullaby and classical music on physiologic stability of hospitalized preterm infants: a randomized trial. *Journal of neonatal-perinatal medicine*, *6*(4), 295-301.

Kemper, K. J., & Danhauer, S. C. (2005). Music as therapy. *South Med J*, *98*(3), 282-8.

Van Der Heijden, M. J., Araghi, S. O., Jeekel, J., Reiss, I. K., Hunink, M. M., & Van Dijk, M. (2016). Do hospitalized premature infants benefit from music interventions? A systematic review of randomized controlled trials. *PloS one*, *11*(9), e0161848.

Stouffer, J. W., Shirk, B. J., & Polomano, R. C. (2007). Practice guidelines for music interventions with hospitalized pediatric patients. *Journal of Pediatric Nursing*, 22(6), 448-456.

13. LoveStart: sing to your baby, even you are a bad singer

Ilari, B., & Sundara, M. (2009). Music listening preferences in early life. Journal of Research in Music Education, 56 (4), 357-369

Brand, M. (1985). Lullabies that awaken musicality in infants. *Music Educators Journal*, 71 (7), 28-31.

Custodero, L. A., & Johnson-Green, E. (2003). Passing the cultural torch: Musical experience and musical perenting of infants. *Journal of Research in Music Education*, 51 (2), 102-114.

Ilari, B., Moura, A., & Bourscheidt, L. (2011). Between interactions and commodities: Musical parenting of infants and toddlers in Brazil. *Music Education Research*, 13 (1), 51-67.

Trehub, S. E., Unyk, A. M., Kamenetsky, S. B., Hill, D. S., Trainor, L. J., Henderson, J. L., et al. (1997). Mothers' and fathers' singing to infants. *Developmental Psychology*, 33 (3), 500- 507.

Shenfield, T., Trehub, S. E., & Nakata, T. (2003). Maternal singing modulates infant arousal. *Psychology of Music*, *31*(4), 365-375.

Montemurro, R. N. R. (1996). Singing lullabies to unborn children: experiences in Village Vilamarxant, Spain. *Pre-and Peri-natal Psychology Journal, 11*(1), 9.

Persico, G., Antolini, L., Vergani, P., Costantini, W., Nardi, M. T., & Bellotti, L. (2017). Maternal singing of lullabies during pregnancy and after birth: Effects on mother–infant bonding and on newborns' behaviour. Concurrent Cohort Study. *Women and Birth.*

Cranley, M. S. (1981). Development of a tool for the measurement of maternal attachment during pregnancy. *Nursing research, 30*(5), 281-284.

Davis, M. S., & AKRIDGE, K. M. (1987). The effect of promoting intrauterine attachment in primiparas on postdelivery attachment. *Journal of Obstetric, Gynecologic, & Neonatal Nursing, 16*(6), 430-437.

Alhusen, J. L. (2008). A literature update on maternal-fetal attachment. *Journal of Obstetric, Gynecologic, & Neonatal Nursing, 37*(3), 315-328.

DiPietro, J. A. (2010). Psychological and psychophysiological considerations regarding the maternal–fetal relationship. *Infant and child development, 19*(1), 27-38.

Pastor, D. L. (1981). The quality of mother–infant attachment and its relationship to toddlers' initial sociability with peers. *Developmental Psychology, 17*(3), 326-335.

Suomi, S. J. (2005). Mother-infant attachment, peer relationships, and the development of social networks in rhesus monkeys. *Human Development*, *48*(1-2), 67-79.

Bergman, K., Sarkar, P., Glover, V., & O'Connor, T. G. (2010). Maternal prenatal cortisol and infant cognitive development: moderation by infant–mother attachment. *Biological psychiatry*, *67*(11), 1026-1032.

Wilson, M. E., White, M. A., Cobb, B., Curry, R., Greene, D., & Popovich, D. (2000). Family dynamics, parental-fetal attachment and infant temperament. *Journal of Advanced Nursing*, *31*(1), 204-210.

Branjerdporn, G., Meredith, P., Strong, J., & Garcia, J. (2017). Associations between maternal-foetal attachment and infant developmental outcomes: A systematic review. *Maternal and child health journal*, *21*(3), 540-553.

14. Talk and read to your baby: the start of a favorable home literacy environment

Sheridan, S. M., Knoche, L. L., Kupzyk, K. A., Edwards, C. P., & Marvin, C. A. (2011). A randomized trial examining the effects of parent engagement on early language and literacy: The Getting Ready intervention. *Journal of school psychology*, *49*(3), 361-383.

Durham, R. E., Farkas, G., Hammer, C. S., Tomblin, J. B., & Catts, H. W. (2007). Kindergarten oral language skill: A key variable in the intergenerational transmission of socioeconomic status. *Research in Social Stratification and Mobility*, *25*(4), 294-305.

Niklas, F., & Schneider, W. (2014). Casting the die before the die is cast: The importance of the home numeracy environment for preschool children. *European Journal of Psychology of Education*, 29, 327-345.

Bus, A. G., van IJzendoorn, M. H., & Pellegrini, A. D. (1995). Joint book reading makes for success in learning to read: A metaanalysis on inter-generational transmission of literacy. *Review of Educational Research*, 65, 1-21.

Niklas, F., Nguyen, C., Cloney, D., Tayler, C., & Adams, R. (2016). Self-report measures of the home learning environment in large scale research: Measurement properties and associations with key developmental outcomes. *Learning Environments Research*, 19, 181-202.

Niklas, F., Cohrssen, C., & Tayler, C. (2016). The sooner, the better: Early reading to children. *SAGE Open*, 6(4), 2158244016672715.

Skeide, M. A., & Friederici, A. D. (2016). The ontogeny of the cortical language network. *Nature Reviews Neuroscience*, *17*(5), 323-332.

15. A double-edged sword: the risk of overstimulation

Nijhuis, J. G. (1995). Physiological and Clinical Consequences in Relation to the Development of Fetal. *Fetal development: A psychobiological perspective*, 67.

Lickliter, R. (1990). Premature visual stimulation accelerates intersenory functioning in bobwhite quail neonates. *Developmental psychobiology*, 23(1), 15-27.

Lickliter, R. (1990). Premature visual experience facilitates visual responsiveness in bobwhite quail neonates. *Infant Behavior and Development*, 13(4), 487-496.

Lickliter, R. (1994). Prenatal visual experience alters postnatal sensory dominance hierarchy in bobwhite quail chicks. *Infant Behavior and Development*, 17(2), 185-193.

Sleigh, M. J., & Lickliter, R. (1995). Augmented prenatal visual stimulation alters postnatal auditory and visual responsiveness in bobwhite quail chicks. *Developmental Psychobiology*, 28(7), 353-366.

Sleigh, M. J., & Lickliter, R. (1997). Augmented prenatal auditory stimulation alters postnatal perception, arousal, and survival in bobwhite quail chicks. *Developmental Psychobiology*, *30*(3), 201-212.

Gerhardt, K. J., Pierson, L. L., Huang, X., Abrams, R. M., & Rarey, K. E. (1999). Effects of intense noise exposure on fetal sheep auditory brain stem response and inner ear histology. *Ear and hearing*, *20*(1), 21-32.

Lalande, N. M., Hétu, R., & Lambert, J. (1986). Is occupational noise exposure during pregnancy a risk factor of damage to the auditory system of the fetus?. *American journal of industrial medicine*, 10(4), 427-435.

Kim, H., Lee, M. H., Chang, H. K., Lee, T. H., Lee, H. H., Shin, M. C., ... & Kim, C. J. (2006). Influence of prenatal noise and music on the spatial memory and neurogenesis in the hippocampus of developing rats. *Brain and Development*, 28(2), 109-114.

Kim, C. H., Lee, S. C., Shin, J. W., Chung, K. J., Lee, S. H., Shin, M. S., ... & Kim, K. H. (2013). Exposure to music and noise during pregnancy influences neurogenesis and thickness in motor and somatosensory cortex of rat pups. *International neurourology journal*, 17(3), 107.

Lalande, N. M., Hétu, R., & Lambert, J. (1986). Is occupational noise exposure during pregnancy a risk factor of damage to the auditory system of the fetus?. *American journal of industrial medicine*, *10*(4), 427-435.

Hrubá, D., Kukla, L., & Tyrlik, M. (1999). Occupational risks for human reproduction: ELSPAC Study. European Longitudinal Study of Pregnancy and Childhood. *Central European journal of public health*, *7*(4), 210-215.

Graven, S. N., & Browne, J. V. (2008). Auditory development in the fetus and infant. *Newborn and infant nursing reviews*, *8*(4), 187-193.

Graven, S. (2006). Sleep and brain development. *Clinics in perinatology*, *33*(3), 693-706.

Gerhardt PhD, K. J., & Robert, M. (2000). Fetal exposures to sound and vibroacoustic stimulation. *Journal of Perinatology*, *20*(8).

Reid, V. M., Dunn, K., Young, R. J., Amu, J., Donovan, T., & Reissland, N. (2017). The human fetus preferentially engages with face-like visual stimuli. *Current Biology*.

Appendix

National Institute on Deafness and Other Communication Disorders. I Love What I Hear! Common Sounds. Available at https://www.nidcd.nih.gov/health/i-love-what-i-hear-common-sounds (last accessed 2017-09-05)

State of California. LOUDNESS COMPARISON CHART (dBA). http://www.dot.ca.gov/dist2/projects/sixer/loud.pdf (last accessed 2017-09-05)

Eastern Kentucky University School of Music. Decibel (Loudness) Comparison Chart. http://music.eku.edu/sites/music.eku.edu/files/ekuhealthandsafety.pdf (last accessed 2017-09-05)

ABOUT THE AUTHOR

Chong Chen is a research scientist at the RIKEN Brain Science Institute in Wako, a suburb of Tokyo, Japan. He studied at Hokkaido University, where he obtained a Ph.D. in Medicine and won several academic awards, including the Takakuwa Eimatsu Award.

Chong has been the author of some 20 articles, all of which have been published in professional journals and which cover several aspects of his fields of expertise; neuroscience, psychiatry and psychology.

In addition to these important pieces, Chong has now written five books, including **Fitness Powered Brains: Optimize Your Productivity, Leadership and Performance**, which is ideal for business people, **Plato's Insight: How Physical Exercise Boosts Mental Excellence**, which shows how being physically active can directly correlate to mental ability and a series of three books called **Your Baby's Developing Brain**, which illustrates the recent scientific finding that babies' brains are developing long before they make their entrance into the world.

The three volumes focus on parental mental health, the optimal maternal nutrition and lifestyle and how the intelligent fetus learns and what parents can do to promote its learning.

When he has free time, Chong likes to get some fresh air and exercise by cycling. He also loves playing ping-pong, reads novels and poems and is a huge fan of the Argentine Tango.

As far as the future goes, Chong hopes that he will be able to translate scientific findings into ways that will allow regular people to live better lives. And through his books, he hopes that he can reach a much wider audience.

You can contact Chong Chen and follow what he is writing about at:

https://brainandlife.net

Twitter: @ChongChenBlog

Email: chen@brainandlife.net

Made in the USA
Middletown, DE
17 July 2018